THE
PASSION
OF THE CHRIST

D0110710

THIS SPECIAL EDITION IS PUBLISHED BY
SAMARITAN'S PURSE WITH PERMISSION FROM
HARVEST CHRISTIAN FELLOWSHIP.

THE
PASSION
OF THE CHRIST

A Biblical Guide
GREG LAURIE

A publication of

Riverside, California
WWW.HARVEST.ORG

Greg Laurie pastors Harvest Christian Fellowship (one of America's largest churches) in Riverside, California. He is the author of several books, including the Gold Medallion Award winner, *The Upside-Down Church,* as well as *Wrestling with God* and *Breakfast with Jesus.*

He is the host of *A New Beginning* radio program and the founder and featured speaker for Harvest Crusades—contemporary, large-scale evangelistic outreaches, which local churches organize nationwide.

Laurie has appeared on *ABC World News Tonight,* Fox News, and MSNBC, sharing how the Bible is relevant for people today. He also serves as a board member for the Billy Graham Evangelistic Association and Samaritan's Purse.

The Passion of the Christ: a Biblical Guide

Text © 2004 by Greg Laurie and Harvest Ministries. All rights reserved.

Designed by Harvest Design

Edited and Researched by Harvest Publications

www.harvest.org

ISBN 1-59328-016-5
Previous ISBN 1-932778-00-4

Printed in the United States of America

CONTENTS

"No one takes it [my life] from Me,

but I lay it down of Myself.

I have power to lay it down,

and I have power to take it again."

※

John 10:18 NKJV

PREFACE: THE POWER
OF THE PASSION

"LET ME MAKE THIS CLEAR: JESUS' DEATH
WAS NO ACCIDENT.
HE WAS BORN TO DIE."

A number of years ago I had the privilege of having lunch with the famed evangelist, Billy Graham. Ruth, his wife, made a classic southern lunch: fried chicken, collard greens—the works. It was one of my first times meeting personally with Billy. I was a little nervous and didn't know what to say. I had all of these questions swimming through my mind. But I finally turned to him and said, "Billy, if you knew as a younger preacher what you know today, would you emphasize anything more as a younger preacher that you find yourself emphasizing today?"

Without missing a beat, he responded, "I would preach more on the cross and on the blood. That is where the power is." I took note of that. I have remembered that to this very day. There is power in the message of the cross, in the shed blood of Jesus Christ.

This power Billy Graham spoke of is the message of Mel Gibson's new movie, *The Passion of The Christ*. It chronicles the last twelve hours of the Lord's life and ministry, starting at the Garden of Geth-semane and following Him through His trial with Pontius Pilate and up to the Crucifixion and Resurrection.

The Passion of The Christ is difficult to watch at times because of its graphic nature, but it is also deeply moving because it is true. It's the true story about how God became a man and intentionally suffered and died on a cross for humanity's sins. Let me make this clear: Jesus' death was no accident. He was born to die. Hundreds of years before Christ's virgin birth, Scripture tells us the Christ would be born of a virgin, "Look! The virgin will conceive a child! She will give birth to a son and will call him Immanuel—'God with us.' " (Isaiah 7:14). The Bible also predicts His death over and over again in the Psalms and in the Prophets (see Psalm 22:1, 16-18; Isaiah 53:12; Zechariah 12:10). It was clearly Jesus Christ's purpose to fulfill the Scriptures by being crucified for the sins of humankind.

There is power in the message of Jesus' crucifixion. Yes, it is arrest-ing. Yes, it is controversial. To some, it is even offensive. But it is the absolute truth. And it is a message often neglected today.

Because of that neglect, many people do not understand the sig-nificance of what took place on that Roman cross two thousand years ago. This is why we at Harvest Ministries have developed this resource, *The Passion of the Christ: a Biblical Guide.* It is my hope and prayer that it will help you know God better through the story of His Passion, and that you'll utilize it as a tool to share the message of the cross. Because that is where the power is.

HOW TO USE THIS BIBLICAL GUIDE

We at Harvest Ministries desire *The Passion of the Christ: a Biblical Guide* to be an easy-to-use reference for your spiritual growth.

Alphabetical Order of Topics

In the chapters "People of the Passion" and "Places of the Passion," each topic is listed alphabetically for quick and simple referencing.

Cross-references

To help you easily find information in this biblical guide, we have provided you with two forms of cross-references:

1. You will encounter asterisks(*) after the first entry of key topics found elsewhere in the chapter you are reading. These asterisks appear to let you know you can read another article on this topic in the same chapter. For example: "Herod Antipas*" directs you to another section in "People of the Passion" entitled "Herod Antipas."

2. You will find cross-references within parentheses by topics that also are discussed in other chapters of this biblical guide. For example: "Garden of Gethsemane (see 'Places of the Passion')" lets you know that this topic is discussed within another chapter called "Places of the Passion." However, due to the frequency in which the name *Jesus Christ* is mentioned, we have avoided cross-referencing, in this manner, every ocurrence of the Lord's name.

"'Are You then the Son of God?'

So He said to them,

'You rightly say that I am.'"

————⚬⚬⚬————

Luke 22:70 NKJV

INTRODUCTION: WHY CHRIST HAD TO DIE

"CHRIST SUFFERED AND DIED ON THE CROSS
FOR NUMEROUS REASONS. BUT
THE SIMPLEST REASON IS HE LOVED US."

*P*ASSION pas_sion \ `pa-sh_n\ n [ME, fr. AF, fr. LL *passion-*,
passio suffering, being acted upon, fr. L *pati* to suffer—more
at PATIENT] (13c) 1 *often cap* a: the sufferings of Christ between the
night of the Last Supper and his death. (*Merriam Webster's Colle-
giate Dictionary*, 11th ed., s.v. "Suffering.")

Ever since I was a small child, I have always had a great admiration
for the historical person known as Jesus Christ (see "People of the
Passion"). I had seen the movies Hollywood had made about His
life. But the one thing I didn't like about the story of Jesus was how
it ended. I used to think, *Whoever wrote the story of Jesus ought
to rewrite it again with a happier ending. This whole story of His
crucifixion should be edited out. It's just not the way His life should
have ended.* You may understand why I would think such a thing.
It seemed to me that Jesus was on something of a roll, after all. He
was healing and teaching people. Little children were flocking to
Him. Clearly, His popularity was growing by leaps and bounds. But

then the unexpected occurred. Jesus was murdered. It is no wonder some people think to themselves, *Why do they have to put Jesus on a cross and kill Him? What a tragic and unnecessary ending to such a wonderful life*!

Becoming a Christian radically transformed my opinion on the ending of Jesus Christ's story. After reading the Gospel accounts for the first time in my life, I began to see that the crucifixion of Jesus was really the primary reason He came to this earth in the first place. The Crucifixion does not read like a storybook ending, because it does not come from the pages of a storybook. It is no mere fairytale. It is a historically true, real-life story, recorded in the pages of Scripture. And the Bible gives us real-life reasons Jesus had to die on the cross.

Christ suffered and died on the cross for numerous reasons. But the simplest reason is He loved us. The Apostle John said it well when he wrote, "This is real love. It is not that we loved God, but that he loved us and sent his Son as a sacrifice to take away our sins" (1 John 4:10). God's love for us and His desire to make right our relationship with Him was why Jesus humbled Himself by becoming a man and dying on the cross for our sins (see Philippians 2:5-11).

To demonstrate the passion behind Christ's love, here are four reasons He died on the cross:

───✿───

- to bring us into a right relationship with God (see Colossians 1:19-20; 2 Corinthians 5:18). Our sin had separated us from God. In order to restore our relationship with God, He sent His Son,

Jesus Christ, to pay the penalty for our sins. That penalty was the cross. With the death and Resurrection, we can now have that right and holy relationship with God by grace through faith in Jesus Christ (see Ephesians 2:8-9).

• to forgive us of our sins and the guilt that accompanied them. In the Hebrew Scriptures, the shed blood of animals was symbolic of the forgiveness of sins. The Bible makes it clear that without this shedding of blood, we cannot be forgiven of our sins (see Hebrews 9:22). Jesus then came to die as a once-and-for-all sacrifice to forgive us of our sins and free us from its guilt (see Acts 13:39).

• to satisfy the radical requirement of the holiness of God (see Leviticus 11:44). God's holiness made a penalty for sin necessary. God's love endured that penalty for the sinner and made payment of the penalty possible. Jesus paid that penalty by experiencing God's wrath and separation from Him on the cross (see Romans 5:9-10; Hebrews 10:12). He was forsaken of God so we don't have to be. He was forsaken for a time that we might enjoy God's presence forever (see Matthew 27:46; see also Hebrews 10:12-14).

• to perform the righteous requirements of the law (see Matthew 3:15; 5:17; Galatians 4:4; 1 Corinthians 1:30). Jesus, through His holy life and suffering on the cross, lived the

3

perfect life we were required to live and took the punishment that we deserved.

These are just some of the reasons Jesus Christ died. But the Apostle Paul summed up the message of the Passion best when he wrote, "[Christ] died for us so that we can live with him forever . . ." (1 Thessalonians 5:10). Clearly, Jesus' death was no ridiculous ending. The cross did not ruin everything. Jesus' death and resurrection saved us from our ruin and gave us life everlasting. This is why we must not blame the people of that day for executing Jesus. Scripture provides no room for anti-Semitism and no room for hatred. Our sins put Him on that cross two thousand years ago. The ending of the Passion of the Christ is the beginning of the happiest story ever told. It is the story of how God became a man so He could die for our sins and so we could be friends with Him once again. He did it for you and He did it for me. All that is left up to us is to believe in Him (see Romans 3:22).

"But the Scriptures

must be fulfilled."

————— ✖✖✖ —————

Mark 14:49 NKJV

THE PROPHECIES OF
THE PASSION

"PROPHECY IS A PERSON OF GOD SPEAKING,
PROCLAIMING, OR ANNOUNCING A MESSAGE UNDER
THE INFLUENCE OF GOD'S INSPIRATION."

*T*he word *prophecy* refers to the God-given message of the prophet. Prophets were people of God who experienced a special encounter with God where He would directly convey a message to them. This encounter would take place through external and internal voices, dreams, and visions, just to name a few. God's message of His will to the prophets varied from judgment, salvation, assurance, and sometimes even future events.

Whatever the content, prophecy is a person of God speaking, proclaiming, or announcing a message under the influence of God's inspiration. It is God's authoritative word to His people.

Included below are some of the prophecies that predicted the Passion of the Christ, made hundreds of years before the Crucifixion.

THE CHRIST'S TRIUMPHAL ENTRY

PROPHESIED: Zechariah 9:9
FULFILLED: Matthew 21:1-11; Mark 11:1-11; Luke 19:28-40;
John 12:12-19

In the Old Testament, the prophet Zechariah called attention to the long-awaited King, the Christ. This king is not like the many wicked kings Israel lived under. He is righteous and humble, so humble that He rides upon a donkey instead of a horse (an animal associated with warfare).

All four Gospel writers record Jesus formally entering into Jerusalem.

THE CHRIST WOULD BE BETRAYED BY A CLOSE FRIEND (Judas Iscariot)

PROPHESIED: Psalm 41:9
FULFILLED: Luke 22:47-48

Judas Iscariot (see "People of the Passion") was one of the twelve disciples that Jesus Christ (see "People of the Passion") called to be close to Him. As the manager of the group's assets, Judas was known for pilfering money. Judas singled out Jesus with a kiss of betrayal in the Garden of Gethsemane (see "Places of the Passion").

BETRAYED FOR THIRTY PIECES OF SILVER

PROPHESIED: Zechariah 11:12-13

FULFILLED: Matthew 26:14-15

Just as the prophet Zechariah foretold, Judas Iscariot (see "People of
the Passion") betrayed Jesus Christ to the religious leaders for thirty
pieces of silver, the price of a slave in those days.

THE CHRIST WOULD BE SCOURGED
AND SPAT UPON

PROPHESIED: Isaiah 50:6
FULFILLED: Matthew 26:67; 27:26

Jesus Christ was spat upon, an act showing contempt and scorn.
As punishment, Jesus' accusers beat Him with a "cat-o'-nine tails," a
whip that was made of cords fastened to a handle with bits of bone
and/or metal attached to it.

THE CHRIST'S BLOOD MONEY WOULD BE USED
TO BUY A POTTER'S FIELD

PROPHESIED: Zechariah 11:12-13
FULFILLED: Matthew 27:9-10

Judas Iscariot, the betrayer, flung the "blood money" on the Temple
(see "Places of the Passion") floor after declaring he had betrayed
innocent blood. The high priests decided to use the money to buy a
field, known as the Potter's Field (See "Places of the Passion"), where
discarded pottery was thrown, to use as a burial place for strangers.

THE CHRIST WOULD BE CRUCIFIED BETWEEN TWO THIEVES

PROPHESIED: Isaiah 53:12
FULFILLED: Matthew 27:38; Mark 15:27-28; Luke 22:37

Two criminals, convicted of robbery, were crucified at the same time as Jesus Christ. The Romans crucified one criminal on the right of Jesus and crucified the other criminal on a cross to the left of Jesus.

THE CHRIST WOULD BE GIVEN VINEGAR TO DRINK

PROPHESIED: Psalm 69:21
FULFILLED: Matthew 27:34, 48; John 19:28-30

After Jesus Christ said, "I thirst," He was offered wine to drink that was mingled with gall. This drink was used to numb the pain of the person being crucified. After tasting it, Jesus refused it, not wanting to take anything that would diminish the pain He came to experience for our sins.

THE CHRIST WOULD SUFFER THE PIERCING OF HIS HANDS AND FEET

PROPHESIED: Psalm 22:16; Zechariah 12:10
FULFILLED: Mark 15:25; John 19:34, 37; 20:25-27

In crucifixions, the victim was most likely affixed to the cross while it was lying on the ground. In Roman crucifixions, the victim's hands were nailed or bound to the cross with their arms extended and raised up. The feet of the crucified were nailed with one or two spikes. Jesus Christ's accusers nailed both His hands and feet to the Roman cross.

———&&&———

THE CHRIST'S GARMENTS WOULD BE DIVIDED AND GAMBLED FOR

PROPHESIED: Psalm 22:18
FULFILLED: Luke 23:34; John 19:23-24

The Roman soldiers nearest the cross divided the garments of Jesus, except for His seamless tunic. They instead decided to cast lots to see who would get the whole garment.

———&&&———

THE CHRIST WOULD BE SURROUNDED AND RIDICULED BY HIS ENEMIES

PROPHESIED: Psalm 22:7-8
FULFILLED: Matthew 27:39-44; Mark 15:29-32

Along with the chief priests, scribes, and elders, were the people passing by who hurled abuse at Jesus Christ. Even the two criminals on the crosses (see "People of the Passion") were casting insults at Him before one of them put his faith in Christ.

THE CHRIST WOULD THIRST

PROPHESIED: Psalm 22:15
FULFILLED: John 19:28

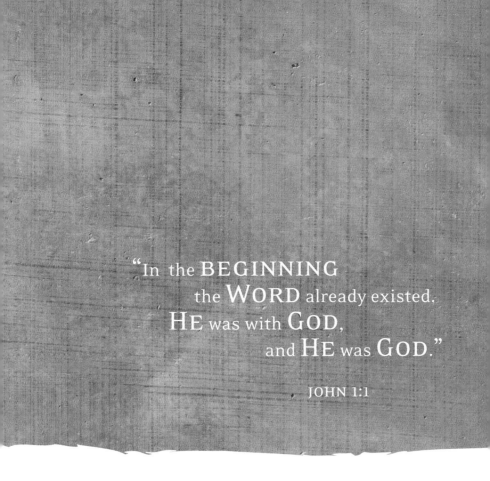

"In the BEGINNING the WORD already existed. HE was with GOD, and HE was GOD."

JOHN 1:1

Jesus Christ displayed His humanity when he experienced physical needs on the cross. His deity did not lessen the brutal and horrific treatment brought upon Him as He suffered on the cross for the sins of all humankind.

THE CHRIST WOULD COMMEND HIS SPIRIT TO THE FATHER

PROPHESIED: Psalm 31:5
FULFILLED: Luke 23:46

Jesus Christ willingly committed Himself to His Father after He had finished all that was required for sinners to have forgiveness and removal of their sins.

THE CHRIST'S BONES WOULD NOT BE BROKEN

PROPHESIED: Exodus 12:46; Numbers 9:12; Psalm 34:20
FULFILLED: John 19:33-36

Oftentimes to hasten the death of the crucified, the soldiers would break the legs of the victim so that suffocation would occur, resulting in death. Jesus was already dead when the soldiers came to perform this act on Him, so there was no need to break any of His bones.

THE CHRIST WOULD BE FORSAKEN BY GOD

PROPHESIED: Psalm 22:1
FULFILLED: Matthew 27:46

On the cross, Jesus Christ cried out, asking God why He had forsaken Him. Many believe it was at this time that fellowship was severed between God the Father and God the Son. The cause of this severed fellowship was the sin of the world falling upon Jesus as He paid the price for humanity's sin. Jesus revealed this separation of intimacy by using the name *God* instead of His more often used and more intimate term *Father.*

⸺⸙⸺

THE CHRIST WOULD BE BURIED WITH THE RICH

PROPHESIED: Isaiah 53:9
FULFILLED: Matthew 27:57-60

Joseph of Arimathea (see "People of the Passion"), a disciple of Jesus Christ, went to Pontius Pilate (see "People of the Passion") and asked to have Jesus' body so he could provide Him with a proper Jewish burial.

⸺⸙⸺

THE CHRIST WOULD ASCEND TO HEAVEN

PROPHESIED: Psalm 24:7-10
FULFILLED: Mark 16:19; Luke 24:51

Forty days after His resurrection, Jesus Christ ascended to heaven to be with the Father.

⸺⸙⸺

THE CHRIST WOULD BE SEATED AT GOD'S RIGHT HAND

PROPHESIED: Psalm 110:1
FULFILLED: Matthew 22:44; Hebrews 10:12-13

The right hand was always a symbol of honor and strength, the supreme seat of authority. The fact the Father exalted Jesus Christ to this place signifies that the risen Christ fulfilled all that was required of Him.

THE CHRIST PREDICTS THE CRUCIFIXION AND RESURRECTION

BESIDES PROPHECIES MADE HUNDREDS OF YEARS BEFORE JESUS CHRIST WAS BORN, JESUS MADE PREDICTIONS CONCERNING HIS OWN DEATH AND RESURRECTION. LISTED BELOW ARE THOSE PREDICTIONS AND THE FULFILLMENTS OF THEM.

THE CHRIST'S FIRST PREDICTION OF HIS DEATH AND RESURRECTION

PREDICTED: Matthew 16:21-28; Mark 8:31-39; Luke 9:21-34
FULFILLED: Matthew 27-28; Mark 15-16; Luke 23-24; John 19-20

THE CHRIST'S SECOND PREDICTION OF HIS DEATH AND RESURRECTION

PREDICTED: Matthew 20:17-29; Mark 10:32-34; Luke 18:31-34
FULFILLED: Matthew 27-28; Mark 15-16; Luke 23-24; John 19-20

THE CHRIST'S THIRD PREDICTION OF HIS DEATH AND RESURRECTION

PREDICTED: Matthew 26:2-5; Mark 14:1-9
FULFILLED: Matthew 27-28; Mark 15-16; Luke 23-24; John 19-20

Much to the surprise and dismay of the disciples, Jesus Christ predicted to them His soon coming suffering, death, and resurrection. He later fulfilled His words when He was crucified, buried, and raised from the dead on the third day.

"*Then he said to Jesus,*

'Lord, remember me when You

come into Your kingdom.'"

⸺

Luke 23:42 NKJV

THE PEOPLE OF
THE PASSION

WHEN THE ROMAN OFFICER WHO STOOD FACING [JESUS]
SAW HOW HE HAD DIED, HE EXCLAIMED,
"TRULY, THIS WAS THE SON OF GOD!" (MARK 15:39)

ANNAS, THE FORMER HIGH PRIEST

Annas was a former high priest (A.D. 6–15) and father-in-law to Joseph Caiaphas,* the high priest during the time of Jesus Christ.* The Gospels continue to refer to Annas as high priest due to his continued power after his official term in office.

In a gesture of respect and acknowledgment of Annas' influence, Caiaphas had Annas begin the preliminary hearings of Christ (see John 18:13). It was there that Annas questioned Christ and then sent Him bound to Caiaphas, the high priest (see John 18:24). Ultimately, Annas was simply a political pawn as his reputation added potential credibility to the unjust plot to kill Jesus Christ.

———

BARABBAS

Barabbas was a known revolutionary convicted of murder during an insurrection in Jerusalem against the Roman and provincial Jewish government (see Luke 23:19).

Barabbas' only appearance in the Passion of the Christ was in Pontius Pilate's* trial of Jesus Christ.* It was there that Pilate tried to free Christ by the means of what is known as the Passover privilege, where the crowd was allowed the option of choosing one prisoner to be set free. When Pilate offered the option of releasing Jesus, the crowds shouted, "Kill him, and release Barabbas to us!" (Luke 23:18). Pilate appeased the crowds and released Barabbas, leaving Jesus to be scourged and then crucified.

―∞∞―

THE CRIMINALS ON THE CROSSES

Jesus Christ* was crucified with two criminals, one on His left side and the other on His right side. One of these convicted criminals joined Jesus' scoffers by saying, "So you're the Messiah, are you? Prove it by saving yourself—and us, too, while you're at it!" (Luke 23:39). Just then, the other criminal protested, explaining that he and the other criminal deserved death for their evil deeds, but Jesus, however, was innocent. This criminal then looked to Jesus and said, "Jesus, remember me when you come into your Kingdom" (Luke 23:42). Jesus replied, "I assure you, today you will be with me in paradise" (Luke 23:43).

The believing criminal is a testimony that forgiveness of sins is not based on any work of our own, for he was a convicted criminal—and not a saint. Instead, our salvation is based on God's grace through our faith in Him (see Ephesians 2:8-9).

HEROD ANTIPAS

Son of Herod the Great, Herod Antipas, or Herod the Tetrarch, ruled over the regions of Galilee and Perea from 4 B.C. to A.D. 39. Antipas was famous for beheading John the Baptist, something the people of his jurisdiction resented (see Matthew 14:3-12; Mark 6:17-29; Luke 3:19-20).

Herod Antipas' role in the Passion of the Christ is small but significant. For various political reasons and in an attempt to escape having to try Jesus Christ,* Pontius Pilate* (Roman Governor of Judea) handed over Jesus to Antipas to be tried, since Jesus was from Antipas' territory of Galilee. Antipas questioned and mocked Jesus, dressing Him in a royal robe, but made no judgment. Antipas then sent Jesus back to Pilate for trial, in fear that Pilate would report him to the emperor.

JESUS CHRIST

Jesus of Nazareth was God's promised Christ (anointed one), who came to die for the sins of the world (see John 3:16). The Gospel of John tells us Jesus existed in the beginning of time and was with God and was God (see John 1:1). Jesus Christ was therefore fully God and fully man. He was born of a virgin in Bethlehem and raised in Nazareth. He grew up like a normal person, raised by His parents Mary and Joseph. But unlike the rest of us, Jesus lived a sinless life. He did, however, experience the temptations that everyday people encounter in everyday life (see Matthew 4).

Jesus began His public ministry at the age of thirty. He ministered largely in Judea, Samaria, and Galilee, and was arrested in Jerusalem, where He died on the cross. His ministry consisted of the calling of the twelve apostles, healing the sick, raising the dead, refuting many of the religious leaders, and preaching the kingdom of God and the repentance of sins.

His ministry came to its climax with His death by crucifixion. Many of Jesus' followers expected Him to overthrow the Roman government and restore the nation of Israel. This, however, was not Jesus' purpose. His Passion was not political, but spiritual. The Passion of the Christ was to reconcile humankind with God by dying for their sins.

Christ ushered in His Passion with the triumphal entry in Jerusalem. There in Jerusalem, Christ was arrested, unjustly tried, and sentenced to die on the cross. Three days later, Jesus fulfilled the Scriptures and rose from the dead. Jesus Christ therefore conquered sin and death and provided a way for all of humankind to be reconciled to God.

JOHN, THE APOSTLE

John is best known as the disciple whom Jesus Christ* loved (see John 19:26). He also was one of the key leaders of the early church, so much so that the Apostle Paul referred to him as one of the three "pillars of the church" (Galatians 2:9). In the Passion, John was the only disciple loyal enough to stay and witness Christ's crucifixion. It was at the foot of the cross that Jesus commissioned John to watch over His mother Mary. After the Resurrection, John was the first of the Twelve to see the empty tomb.

—∞∞—

JOSEPH OF ARIMATHEA

In the Passion of the Christ, Joseph of Arimathea was a member of the Sanhedrin* and a secret follower of Christ who paid respect and honor to Christ by providing Him with a proper burial. Joseph's provision of a proper burial for Christ is marked by the clean linen with embalming oil in which he and Nicodemus* wrapped Jesus Christ's* body and the new tomb in which he laid Jesus (see Matthew 27:59-60; Luke 23:53; John 19:38-42). Joseph, therefore, helped to provide Christ with a burial fitting for a king.

—∞∞—

JOSEPH CAIAPHAS, THE HIGH PRIEST

Joseph Caiaphas was the high priest from A.D. 18-36/37. He was son in-law to Annas the former high priest.* In the Passion, he was an expert politician who was convinced that Jesus Christ's* death would lead to political peace. After being interrogated by Annas, Jesus was delivered to Caiaphas for a treacherous night-time trial, where Caiaphas and the Jewish leaders attempted to find a false testimony against Jesus (see Matthew 26:59-68; Mark 14:55-65; Luke 22:63-65; John 18:24). When no adequate false testimony was found, Caiaphas asked Jesus if He was the Messiah, the Son of the blessed God (see Mark 14:61). Jesus answered, "I am," and Caiaphas falsely accused Him of blasphemy and stated that Jesus deserved the death sentence (see Matthew 26:65-66;

Mark 14:60-63). Caiaphas was yet another person involved in the unjust trial and conviction of the Christ.

JUDAS ISCARIOT

Judas Iscariot is infamous for being the disciple who betrayed Jesus Christ.* He initiated his betrayal in Bethany when he met with the leading priests to betray Christ for the price of thirty pieces of silver (see Matthew 26:14-16; Mark 14:10-11). Judas finalized the deal by identifying Jesus to His arresters in the Garden of Gethsemane (see "Places of the Passion"), where Jesus was arrested (see Matthew 26:47-50; Mark 14:43-46; Luke 22:47-53; John 18:3-11).

The Gospels do reveal that Judas regretted his actions and went to the leading priests and tried to right his wrong by returning the money and confessing to them that he had "betrayed an innocent man" (Matthew 27:4). The priests, however, rejected the money and would have nothing to do with him. More than likely sickened by the outcome of his actions, Judas threw the money on the floor of the Temple and went out and hung himself (see Matthew 27:5).

MALCHUS, THE HIGH PRIEST'S SERVANT

At the arrest of Jesus Christ,* Peter,* in an attempt to free Jesus, cut off Malchus' ear with a sword. Jesus then commanded Peter to put away his sword, reminding Peter that He was supposed to die for humankind (see John 18:11; Matthew 26:51-56). Jesus then touched Malchus' ear and healed it (see Luke 22:51).

MARY MAGDALENE

Mary Magdalene was a follower of Jesus Christ* from the time He began visiting cities and villages to announce the Good News of the kingdom of God (see Luke 8:1-2). Unlike most of the disciples, Mary is found following Christ closely throughout the final day of the Passion. She is found watching the Crucifixion (see Mark 15:40), standing by the cross of Jesus (see John 19:25), coming early to visit His tomb with spices (see Mark 16:1; John 20:1), being among the first to see the risen Lord (see Mark 16:9), and lastly, reporting to the disciples about the Resurrection (see Luke 24:10; John 20:18). In the Passion, Mary Magdalene proved to be a devoted follower of Christ, who ministered to Him from beginning to ending.

MARY, THE MOTHER OF JAMES AND JOSEPH

In the Passion of the Christ, Mary (the mother of James and Joseph) is often found with the other female disciples, standing at the foot of the cross, and anointing Jesus Christ* for burial. Like the other women followers, she was a disciple full of deep commitment and faith, willing to stand by Christ at times when few others would.

MARY, THE MOTHER OF JESUS

Mary was a young Jewish virgin engaged to a man named Joseph. God sent the angel Gabriel to tell her she was "blessed among women" (Luke 1:42), because He had privileged her with giving birth to the Savior of the world. In the Passion, Mary is found at the foot of the cross where Jesus Christ* commissioned John, the apostle* to

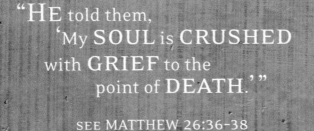

> "HE told them,
> 'My SOUL is CRUSHED
> with GRIEF to the
> point of DEATH.'"

SEE MATTHEW 26:36-38

watch over His mother. After Christ rose from the dead, Mary, along with Jesus' brothers, was among the disciples who awaited Pentecost (see Acts 1:14).

NICODEMUS

Nicodemus was a Pharisee and a member of the Sanhedrin.* He met with Jesus Christ* at night and discussed with Him the need to be born again (see John 3:1-21). He later openly defended Christ before the Sanhedrin. In the Passion, Nicodemus helped Joseph of Arimathea* provide Jesus with a proper burial. Nicodemus was most likely among the many who believed in Christ, but did not confess their belief in fear that they would be excommunicated (see John 12:42). Christian tradition states that Nicodemus was indeed a believer.

PETER

Peter is the famous follower of Jesus Christ* whom the Bible often depicts as the leader of the twelve apostles. Peter's birth name was Simon, but Jesus renamed him Peter, which means "rock." His actions, however, were not always as firm and fast as his name implied. Peter was much like the rest of us, a person who experienced ups and downs in his relationship with Christ, at one moment a success and at other times a failure.

Peter's role in the Passion of the Christ is equally dynamic. At the Last Supper, he boldly protested any possibility that he could deny Jesus, insisting that he would die before ever denying Him (see Matthew 26:35). Tragically, all four Gospel writers depict Peter's three-fold denial of Christ just before His crucifixion (see Matthew 26:69-75; Mark 14:66-72; Luke 22:55-62; John 18:25-27).

Peter's part in the Passion doesn't end in failure, however. After the Resurrection, Jesus appeared to Peter personally (see Luke 24:34) and later restored Peter, telling him, "Follow me" (see John 21:19). Peter's life is proof that he did just that. He was one of the central leaders of the early church and died a martyr's death under Nero's persecution of the Christians.

PONTIUS PILATE

Pontius Pilate was Roman governor (or prefect) of Judea from A.D. 26-36/37 and was a key political figure in the Passion of the Christ. Early Friday morning of the Passion Week, the Jewish leaders brought Jesus Christ* before Pontius Pilate, accusing Him of claiming to be king. Pilate desired to release Jesus because of His innocence, knowing the chief priests handed over Jesus due to envy. The crowds, however, were relentless at Christ's trial, demanding for Him to be crucified. Pilate then gave in and took water and washed his hands clean, saying "I am innocent of the blood of this man. The responsibility is yours!" (Matthew 27:24). The crowds yelled in agreement and Pilate had Jesus scourged and handed over for crucifixion. Shortly after Christ's crucifixion, Pilate was recalled from office. Christian tradition states that he later committed suicide.

PONTIUS PILATE'S WIFE

Claudia Procula, Pontius Pilate's* wife, appeared on the scene of the Passion during the trial of Christ. Just as Pilate was attempting to free Christ, she sent him a message concerning Jesus Christ.* The message read: "Don't have anything to do with that innocent man, for I have suffered a great deal today in a dream because of him" (Matthew 27:19). Despite her wise counsel, Pilate gave in to the wishes of the crowds and had Jesus scourged and crucified.

THE ROMAN CENTURION

The Roman centurion in the Passion was so impressed by Jesus

Christ's* death that he made the statement, "Truly, this was the Son of God!" (Mark 15:39). The centurion's words may have been a profession of faith in Christ or he may have simply meant that Jesus was a righteous and innocent man, as Luke states it (see Luke 23:47). Either way, the Roman centurion's statement is further evidence that the political and religious leaders of the day were guilty of crucifying the innocent Christ, who was indeed the Son of God.

SALOME

Salome was a faithful follower of Jesus Christ* and helped care for Him while He was in Galilee. In the Passion, Salome is seen at the foot of the cross with Mary Magdalene* and Mary, the mother of James and Joseph* (see Mark 15:41). After Christ's death, Salome, along with Mary Magdalene and Mary, the mother of James, brought spices to anoint Christ's body for burial (see Mark 16:1). Salome is an example of a loving and faithful follower of Christ who helped care for Him even when most deserted Him.

THE SANHEDRIN

The Sanhedrin was the supreme Jewish council in Jerusalem during the times of the New Testament. It presided over the religious, political, and legal issues of all Jews. The Sanhedrin's membership consisted of seventy-one Jewish leaders. The head of the Sanhedrin was the high priest (see Matthew 26:57). After Herod the Great's reign, religious reasons ceased to be the primary means for choosing the high priest. More often than not, he was appointed for political reasons. Under the high priest was the captain of the Temple (see Luke 22:4, 52). The rest of the members were select Levites and priests. The Bible seems to point to the chief priests, former high priests who belonged to the Sadducees, as the central members of the Sanhedrin (see Acts 4:1; 5:17). The Gospels provide evidence that Pharisees were members of the Sanhedrin as well (see John 3:1). In the Passion, the Sanhedrin was partly responsible for the planning and carrying out of Christ's trial (see Matthew 26:59; Mark 14:55; 15:1; John 11:47-53).

SATAN

Satan was an exalted angelic being who became proud and attempted to dethrone God (see Isaiah 14:12-14; Ezekiel 28:11-19). God, who is in control of all things, removed Satan from his position of honor. Satan then convinced one-third of the angels to follow him in his mission to usurp the plans of God.

Although Satan played a part in tempting both Judas Iscariot* and Peter* in the Passion of the Christ (see Luke 22:3; Luke 22:31), the Crucifixion was not the result of Satan's doing. It was Jesus Christ's* intended purpose to die on the cross for the sins of the world (see John 3:16).

SIMON OF CYRENE

Simon was from Cyrene, a district of North Africa. On the road to Golgotha (see "Places of the Passion"), the Romans forced Simon to carry Jesus Christ's* cross in the Passion (see Matthew 27:32; Mark

"They made a CROWN of long, SHARP THORNS and put it on HIS HEAD ...."

MATTHEW 27:29

15:21; Luke 23:26). Simon was the father of Alexander and Rufus. In his letter to the Romans, the Apostle Paul said Rufus was chosen of the Lord; he also stated that Rufus' mother, perhaps Simon's wife, had been a mother to him as well (see Romans 16:13). From Paul's words, we can presume Simon may have later become a Christian.

"Taking Jesus' body

down from the cross,

he wrapped it

in the cloth

and laid it

in the tomb . . . . "

Mark 15:46

THE PLACES OF
THE PASSION

AND THEY BROUGHT JESUS TO A PLACE CALLED
GOLGOTHA (WHICH MEANS SKULL HILL). . . . THEN THEY
NAILED HIM TO THE CROSS. (MARK 15:22, 24a)

THE GARDEN OF GETHSEMANE

After the Last Supper, Jesus Christ (see "People of the Passion")
and His disciples went to a place called the Garden of Gethsemane,
located on the slopes of the Mount of Olives* (see Luke 22:39). Gethsemane was probably in an olive grove, containing an olive press.
In the Passion, Jesus took His disciples to Gethsemane to pray in
preparation for His crucifixion. Peter, James, and John fell asleep
instead of praying, even despite Jesus' passionate prayer for the
Father's will to be done (see Luke 22:39-46).

When Jesus finished His prayer and awoke the disciples, Judas
Iscariot (see "People of the Passion") appeared with a mob to arrest
Christ. Judas then kissed Christ as a prearranged signal so they
would know whom to arrest (see Matthew 26:47-49). During the
arrest, Peter (see "People of the Passion") cut off the ear of Malchus,
the high priest's servant (see "People of the Passion"). But Jesus

healed Malchus' ear and reminded Peter that He must be arrested and crucified in order to fulfill the Scriptures (see Matthew 26:51-54; John 18:10-11).

THE GARDEN TOMB

The Garden Tomb was the burial site of Jesus Christ. Unlike tombs today, this tomb was carved out of a rock with the entrance covered by a large stone. Luke, in his Gospel, tells us that it was a new tomb where no one ever had been laid (see Luke 23:53).

GOLGOTHA (CALVARY)

Jesus Christ was crucified between two criminals at Golgotha. It was located on an elevated site somewhere near Jerusalem and close to the Garden Tomb,* where Jesus was buried (see Matthew 27:33; Mark 15:22; John 19:17, 41). The Bible also refers to Golgotha as Calvary, which means "Skull Hill."

MOUNT OF OLIVES

In His final week, Jesus Christ taught on the Mount of Olives and spent His nights there as well (see Mark 13; Luke 21:37). The Mount of Olives is a rounded hill reaching 2,676 feet high and overlooked the Temple.* After the Last Supper, Jesus brought His disciples to the Mount of Olives, where they prayed nearby in the Garden of Gethsemane.* Immediately after praying, Jesus was betrayed by Judas and arrested at Gethsemane. The Mount of Olives also was the location where the disciples witnessed Christ's ascension (see Acts 1:9-12).

THE POTTER'S FIELD

This was the field the leading priests purchased with the thirty pieces of silver that Judas Iscariot (see "People of the Passion") returned to them. The priests were not able to return the money to the Temple* treasury because it had been used to pay for murder (see Matthew 27:1-10). Instead, they bought the Potter's Field with the money, and used it as a cemetery for foreigners.

THE PRAETORIUM

The Praetorium was the residence of Pontius Pilate, governor of Rome (see "People of the Passion"). It was here that Pilate questioned Jesus Christ before His crucifixion (see John 18:28). The word *praetorium* also can loosely refer to another part of the residence, such as where the Roman soldiers mocked Jesus after appearing before Pilate (see Matthew 27:27-31; Mark 15:16-20).

THE RESIDENCE AND COURTYARD OF CAIAPHAS AND ANNAS

Joseph Caiaphas, the high priest, and Annas, the former high priest (see "People of the Passion") lived in different wings of the same residence. In the courtyard of this residence was where Peter's (see "People of the Passion") denial took place while Annas interrogated

Jesus inside the residence. Annas then sent Jesus to Caiaphas for trial, which occurred in another area of the home (see Matthew 26:57-58; Mark 14:53-54; Luke 22:54-55; John 18:19-24).

THE TEMPLE

The Temple at Jerusalem, which Herod the Great constructed, was the center of religious and social life for Jews of Jesus Christ's day. It was an ornate, cream-colored house of worship that filled an area measuring approximately 490 yards from north to south and 325 yards from east to west. Significant events occurred there such as Jesus' cleansing of the moneychangers and His preaching about the coming destruction of the Temple.

THE UPPER ROOM

In biblical times, upper rooms were second-story rooms of homes that looked like towers. In the Passion, Jesus Christ and His disciples ate the Passover supper in an upper room. The disciples returned there after Jesus' resurrection and ascension as they waited for Pentecost.

"The chief priests

had handed Him over

because of envy."

⬦⬦⬦

Mark 15:10 NKJV

THE POLITICS OF
THE PASSION

"JESUS' PURPOSE WAS NOT TO LIBERATE THE JEWISH PEOPLE
OF POLITICAL OPPRESSION, BUT TO LIBERATE ALL PEOPLE FROM
SIN'S RULE OVER HUMANKIND."

*S*imilar to the politics that we know of today, the politics of
the Passion of the Christ were controversial and overflowing
with both evil and good.

By the time of Jesus Christ (see "People of the Passion"), the Jews
were no longer an independent nation. They lived under Roman
rule, and many found themselves hoping for a future Christ (anointed one) who would free them from the political reign of the Romans.

Jesus of Nazareth was the Christ the Jews were hoping for, but He did
not come in the fashion most expected. Jesus' purpose was not to
liberate the Jewish people of political oppression, but to liberate all
people from sin's rule over humankind. Despite His mission to save
the world from sin and reconcile humanity to God (see Colossians
1:19-20), His teachings and actions angered many of the religious-
political leaders of the day.

Jesus' cleansing of the Temple (see "Places of the Passion") provided the main religious reason for His crucifixion. The cleansing symbolized Jesus' rejection of the authorities of the Temple and the systems that supported and improved their control over its religious and social functions. This no doubt angered and threatened the Temple authorities, leading them to plot the death of Jesus.

One problem, however, stood in the path of the religious leaders' plan to kill Christ. Historical sources and tradition tell us Rome had completely taken away from the Jews the right to try capital cases during Jesus' time. Other sources tell us the Jews could not execute the death penalty independent from Roman authority. Whichever case was true, the Jewish leaders were dependent upon the Roman government to execute the Christ. This left the religious leaders with no other choice than to find political reasons to put Jesus to death. Left with little to work with, they falsely charged Jesus with stirring up the people of Rome by telling them not to pay their taxes, and with claiming to be king (see Luke 23:2).

On top of these unjust charges brought against Jesus, His trial also lacked justice and was in violation of Jewish law. In trying Jesus, the religious leaders committed at least five crimes that contradicted Jewish law:

1. assembling for trial in the high priest's residence instead of the Temple (see Matthew 26:3; Mark 14:53-54; Luke 22:54; John 18:13-15)
2. trying Jesus at night instead of by day
3. convening for a trial on the eve of a Sabbath or a feast day

4. reaching a guilty verdict on the same day of the trial
5. sentencing Jesus based on inadequate grounds for blasphemy. Scripture defines *blasphemy* as "one who curses God" (Leviticus 24:15-16), a crime Jesus never committed (see Matthew 26:65; Mark 14:64)

In looking at the above information, some people may falsely blame the Jewish leaders for Jesus' death. But we must remember that the Jewish leaders were not the only people who acted unjustly in the trial and execution of Jesus. The Roman government, through the actions of Pontius Pilate and Herod Antipas (see "People of the Passion"), were also complicit in the death of Christ. Most importantly, we need to realize that Jesus' death was not the result of an unjust and deceitful trial. Nor was any single ethnic or religious group responsible for His trial and crucifixion. It was the sins of human-kind—past, present, and future—that nailed Christ to the cross. The Crucifixion was the passionate plan of God, who longed to reconcile the world to Himself so He and His people could once again have a right and holy relationship with each other.

The New Testament Scriptures tell us, "For God so loved the world that he gave his only Son, so that everyone who believes in him will not perish but have eternal life. God did not send his Son into the world to condemn it, but to save it" (John 3:16-17). You see, God the Father made the ultimate sacrifice of sending His Son, Jesus Christ, in our place to live the most holy life and then to die the most grue-some death for our sins. Why would God do such a thing for us? Because God so loved the world.

THE CHRONOLOGY OF THE PASSION

To help you experience what Jesus Christ went through during the last day of His life, here is a chronology of the final events of the life of Jesus of Nazareth.

KEY EVENTS	TIME OF DAY
Christ and the Disciples Eat the Last Supper	Thurs. Evening
Christ Prays in the Garden of Gethsemane and Is Then Betrayed and Arrested	Thurs. Evening
Annas the Former High Priest Interrogates Christ	Thurs. Night BEFORE MIDNIGHT
Joseph Caiaphas, the High Priest Begins the Formal Trial of Christ	Friday Morning SOMETIME AFTER MIDNIGHT
The High Priest's Questioning of Christ	Friday Morning EARLY
Peter's Denial of Christ	Friday Morning AROUND 3 A.M.
The Mocking of Christ	Friday Morning EARLY
The Jewish Trial Ends with the Sanhedrin's Decision against Christ	Friday Morning AS DAY WAS DAWNING
Christ Is Led to Pontius Pilate and Accused of Sedition	Friday Morning
Judas Iscariot Hangs Himself	Friday Morning
Christ's Initial Hearing before Pontius Pilate	Friday Morning
Pilate Hands Christ over to Herod Antipas; Herod Mocks Christ	Friday Morning
Pontius Pilate and Herod Antipas Are Reconciled	Friday Morning
Pontius Pilate Resumes the Trial of Christ; Christ Is Scourged and Mocked	Friday Morning
Christ on the Road to the Cross	Friday SOMETIME BEFORE 9:00 A.M.
Christ Is Crucified	Friday FROM 9:00 A.M. TO 3:00 P.M.
Christ Is Buried	Friday Evening AS EVENING APPROACHED
Christ in the Tomb	Saturday
Christ Rises from the Dead	Sunday Morning AS NEW DAY WAS DAWNING

The Passion According To...

MATTHEW	MARK	LUKE	JOHN
26:20-29	14:17-25	22:14-38	13:2-4
26:36-56	14:26-52	22:39-53	18:1-12
			18:13
26:57	14:53	22:54	18:24
26:59-68	14:55-65		18:19-24
26:69-75	14:66-72	22:55-62	18:15-18, 25-27
		22:63-65	
27:1	15:1a	22:66-71	
27:2	15:1b	23:1	18:28
27:3-10			
27:11-14	15:2-5	23:2-6	18:29-40
		23:7-11	
		23:12	
27:17-31	15:8-20	23:13-25	19:1-16
27:32-34	15:21-23	23:26-32	19:17
27:35	15:25	23:33	19:18
27:57-61	15:42-47	23:50-55	19:38-42
27:62-65	16:1	23:56	
28:1-15	16:1-8	24:1-35	20:1-18

"*Then Jesus shouted,*

'Father,

I entrust my spirit

into your hands!'

And with those words

he breathed his last."

Luke 23:46

SEVEN STATEMENTS
FROM THE CROSS

GREG LAURIE REVIEWS THE FINAL WORDS
OF JESUS CHRIST.

he seven statements Jesus Christ (see "People of the Passion") made from the cross give us a glimpse into the eternal and show us that our salvation was paid in full, once and for all, at the cross. The final words of the dying capture our attention, often reveal the speaker's character, and can even impart wisdom for our own lives. The final words of Jesus do that and much more.

STATEMENT ONE
"Father, forgive them for they know not what they do."

The fact that Jesus' first words from the cross consisted of a prayer does not surprise us. Jesus always had been a man of prayer.

But we might have expected Jesus to pray, "Father, help me!" Or, even His later statement being His first: "My God, my God, why have you forsaken me?" But Knowing Jesus, it was only fitting that He should say what He said in the very order He said it.

He did not pray, in that dark hour, for His loved ones first or for His friends. He prayed for His enemies! He modeled exactly what He taught.

We also see from this example of Jesus that no one is beyond the reach of prayer. No matter how hopeless it may look, keep praying for that person! It was as if Jesus was saying, "Father, forgive them, for they need forgiveness so desperately. . . . Forgive them, for they have committed a sin that is wicked beyond all comprehension. . . . Forgive them, for they have committed a sin that is black beyond all their realization."

Maybe you're praying for someone right now to see his or her need for God. You've brought that friend to church, but there's no apparent interest in spiritual things. Keep praying!

STATEMENT TWO
"Today you will be with Me in Paradise."

His second statement was an answer to prayer. Next to Jesus were two criminals being crucified. Something significant happened to change the heart of one of these criminals, bringing him to his spiritual senses. Jesus' second statement was an answer to that prayer for forgiveness. Jesus spoke to that criminal as though he were the only person in the world. What joy must have filled this man's heart when he heard these words! We cannot help but notice this man's immediate faith: "Lord, remember me when you come into your Kingdom."

He did not say, "Remember me *if* you come into your Kingdom," but rather, "Remember me *when* you come into your Kingdom" (Luke 23:42, emphasis mine).

It would seem, at this moment, that this thief, who only had come alive spiritually just moments before, had more spiritual insight than many of Jesus' closest followers!

Also, I love the way this new convert defends Jesus to the other: "Don't you fear God even when you are dying? We deserve to die for our evil deeds, but this man hasn't done anything wrong" (Luke 23:40-41).

Amazingly, both men heard these words of Jesus. Both saw His flawless and incredible example. Both were dying, and both needed forgiveness. The unrepentant thief died as he had lived, hardened and indifferent. The other repented, believed, and as a result, joined Jesus in Paradise.

The mystery of the gospel! Hearing the same message, one person will listen with indifference while another will have his or her eyes opened to his or her needs and will believe.

STATEMENT THREE

"Woman, behold your son. . . ."

The Lord's third statement from the cross was a response to what He saw. At the foot of the cross was His mother Mary, along with some

"These things happened in FULFILLMENT of the SCRIPTURES that say, ... 'They will look on HIM whom they PIERCED.'"

JOHN 19:36–37

other women and John, the apostle (see "People of the Passion"). Looking down at Mary and John, He said to His mother, "Woman, behold your son." Then He said to John, "Behold your mother." From that hour, John took Mary into his home. The Lord was think-ing about the needs of His mother and her future on Earth.

STATEMENT FOUR
"My God, My God, why have You forsaken Me?"

At noon, darkness suddenly fell on the earth. Piercing through that darkness was Christ's voice as He cried out, *"Eli, Eli, lama sabachthani?"* (Matthew 27:46; see also Mark 15:34).

It was at this moment that I believe Jesus bore all the sins of the world. Every wicked thing ever done by every person was poured on Jesus at that very moment. In my opinion, it was God's most painful moment.

You would think, as a moment like this was unfolding, that the people would stand in complete silence, especially when darkness fell on the earth. But as we read the crucifixion account, we realize that the mockery continued until the very end. Even as He was bearing the sins of the world and crying out, *"Eli, Eli, lama sabachthani?"* they had no interest at all. People were laughing, mocking, gambling, and acting as though nothing of any importance was taking place. In reality, the most significant event in human history was quickly unfolding.

STATEMENT FIVE
"I thirst!"

We find the next words Jesus gave from the cross in John 19:28-29:

After this, Jesus, knowing that all things were now accomplished, that the Scripture might be fulfilled, said, "I thirst!" Now a vessel full of sour wine was sitting there; and they filled a sponge with sour wine, put it on hyssop, and put it to His mouth. (NKJV)

"I thirst!" was the first from the lips of our Lord of a personal nature. Understand that this was not merely a casual thirst. This was a thirst produced by a tremendous loss of blood. This was a thirst produced by a man who had literally borne the sins of the world. This was a thirst like no man has ever known before. Imagine the Creator of the universe, God Almighty, saying, "I thirst!" The very One who created water was crying out for just a few drops to quench this insatiable thirst.

"I thirst," was a statement Jesus said to the woman at the well when He asked for a drink of water. Again, as He was hanging on the cross, He said, "I thirst." Here is what it comes down to: because Jesus thirsted, we don't have to. Because He died on the cross, we don't have to be thirsty. He has made possible a way for us to know God. No longer do we have to go thirsting after the empty things this world offers. We can satisfy our thirst in a relationship with Him.

You may recall that prior to this moment, Jesus was offered sour wine mingled with gall, basically, a painkiller. You might also remember that the Lord refused it (see Matthew 27:34). He was going to bear the Crucifixion and all of its pain. He would take upon Himself the sin of the world and all of its horror, and He wanted to have full use of His mental faculties.

STATEMENT SIX
"It is finished!"

Now, having borne the sins of the world, Jesus cried out, "It is finished!" (John 19:30). This battle cry of the cross was the greatest and most far-reaching battle cry ever heard in history. Those who stood close, Mary, John, the Roman soldiers, and others, were not the only ones who heard these three words. I believe these words echoed throughout heaven. I am sure they were heard as a cry of victory among the angels who would have, at any moment, come and gladly delivered the Lord from this situation. "It is finished!"

I also think these words reverberated throughout the hallways of hell as Satan (see "People of the Passion") realized his plan had backfired. In his blind rage and jealousy, Satan had filled the heart of Judas Iscariot (see "People of the Passion") to betray the Lord, but he actually helped bring about the crucifixion of Christ. He unwittingly played into the plan and purpose of the Father, who determined long ago that God would come to this earth as a man and die on a cross. It is spoken of extensively in the Old Testament. Suddenly, perhaps at this moment, it dawned on the devil that he just helped fulfill prophetic Scriptures. He helped bring about the purposes of God. What was meant to destroy Jesus would now ultimately destroy the devil.

What does this phrase, "It is finished," mean? It could be translated a number of ways: It is made an end of. It is paid. It is performed. It is accomplished. Each one of these phrases gives a different facet to the meaning of "It is finished!"

WHAT WAS MADE AN END OF?
Our sins and the guilt that accompanied them.

WHAT WAS PAID?
The price of our redemption.

WHAT WAS PERFORMED?
The righteous requirements of the law.

WHAT WAS ACCOMPLISHED?
All that the Father had given Jesus to do.

The storm had finally passed. The devil had done his worst, and the Lord had bruised Him. The darkness had ended, and it was finished. Understand, this was a victory cry from Calvary. This was a glorious moment because the work was now completed.

What was finished? Finished were the horrendous sufferings of Christ. Never again would He experience pain or be in the hands of Satan. Never again would He bear the sins of the world. Never again would He, even for a moment, be forsaken of God. Finished were the demands of the Mosaic Law, those standards laid out in the Scripture that we were unable to keep.

Satan's stronghold on humanity was finished. Because of what Jesus did on the cross, we no longer have to be under the power of Satan.

This does not mean we never will be tempted. It does not mean we are not vulnerable to the enticements of the Wicked One. But it

does mean that Satan has no rights over our lives. We were under his control, but Jesus suffered for our redemption. Jesus came and died on the cross for our freedom. This is what happened for us at Calvary. The humility, the sorrow, the suffering, the separation, the love—that is the Passion of Jesus Christ.

> "'And when I AM LIFTED UP on the CROSS, I will draw EVERYONE to MYSELF.'"
>
> JOHN 12:32

Therefore, we no longer have to be under the power of any sin if we don't want to be. We don't have to be under the power of immorality. We don't have to be under the power of addiction to drugs or alcohol. We don't have to be under the power of any vice or any lifestyle. We have been freed by the work that Jesus performed on the cross. He has opened the door of our prison cells, but each of us must get up and walk out.

Some of us don't really want to be freed from the vice that may have a stranglehold on our lives. Some of us don't want to change. Some of us don't want to get out of the darkness we are in. I am telling you on the authority of Scripture that if you want out, the door is open. Jesus Christ has paid the price. He will give you the power and resources to be victorious over the power of sin. Your life may not be sinless, but you can sin less. Your life can be transformed because of what was finished on the cross.

Finished was our salvation. All our sins were transferred to Jesus when He hung on the cross, and righteousness was transferred to our account. As Isaiah 53:6 says, "The Lord has laid on Him the iniquity of us all" (NKJV). It is finished. There is nothing that you or I can add to the work that Jesus did for us.

It is all paid—no more debts left. Jesus has done this for you and for me. "It is finished!"

STATEMENT SEVEN
"Into Your hands I commit My spirit."

Jesus then gave His seventh and final statement from the cross. He said to the Father, "Into Your hands I commit My spirit" (Luke 23:46 NKJV). The Lord often said, "No one takes it [my life] from Me, but I lay it down of Myself. I have power to lay it down, and I have power to take it again" (John 10:18 NKJV). The Roman soldiers who came to break Jesus' legs were amazed that He already had died. This practice was intended to prevent the one on the cross from pulling up for a breath. As a result, the prisoner would immediately die of suffocation. When they came to Jesus, it was not necessary to break His bones, which fulfilled the Scriptures that said not one of His bones would be broken (see Exodus 12:46; Numbers 9:12; Psalm 34:20; John 19:36).

THE SEVEN STATEMENTS FROM THE CROSS

CHRIST MADE HIS LOVE FOR THE WORLD PASSIONATELY EVIDENT IN THESE LAST STATEMENTS FROM THE CROSS, AND THE PRESENTATION OF THESE STATEMENTS IN ALL OF THEIR PAIN, VICTORY, AND MEANING IS POWERFUL TO BEHOLD.

⎯⎯⎯

"Father, forgive them for they know not what they do."
DO YOU REALIZE THAT YOU ARE IN NEED OF THE FATHER'S FORGIVENESS?

⎯⎯⎯

"Today you will be with Me in Paradise."
HAVE YOU REALIZED AND CONFESSED JESUS AS YOUR PERSONAL SAVIOR?

"Woman, behold your son."
JESUS IS CONCERNED AND PROVIDES FOR ALL OF US.

———⊗⊗⊗———

"My God, My God, why have You forsaken Me?"
JESUS WAS FORSAKEN SO WE DON'T HAVE TO BE.

———⊗⊗⊗———

"I thirst!"
THIS PERSONAL STATEMENT REMINDS US THAT JESUS IS NOT ONLY GOD, BUT HE ALSO WAS MAN. JESUS IDENTIFIES WITH OUR NEEDS.

———⊗⊗⊗———

"It is finished."
OUR SIN IS PAID FOR AND SIN'S CONTROL OVER OUR LIVES IS BROKEN!

———⊗⊗⊗———

"Into Your hands I commit My spirit."
YOU CAN ENTRUST YOUR LIFE INTO GOD'S HANDS.

"And He said to them,

'Go into all the world

and preach the gospel

to every creature.'"

Mark 16:15 NKJV

SHARING THE GOSPEL OF THE PASSION

"OTHER THAN THE BIBLE AND OUR OWN LIVES, I BELIEVE THAT
The Passion of The Christ MAY WELL BE THE MOST EFFECTIVE
EVANGELISTIC TOOL WE HAVE HAD IN YEARS."

The Passion of The Christ, directed and produced by Academy Award® winner Mel Gibson, is the most effective and powerful visual presentation of the suffering and death of Jesus I have ever seen in my life. But *The Passion of The Christ* is not just a film; it is an evangelistic tool. Other than the Bible and our own lives, I believe that *The Passion of The Christ* may well be the most effective evangelistic tool we have had in years. I believe God's hand is on this film. And I believe that people will come to Christ as a result of seeing it. I said this to Mel Gibson after I saw an unedited screening of the movie for the first time. He was present at the screening, and I told him, "Mel, I don't know if this film is going to be a commercial hit or not, though I suspect it will be, but I believe this film will result in thousands of people coming to Christ."

We, as believers, need to wake up to this opportunity. It may be hard to get your friends to go to church with you, but I suspect they might go to a movie with you. This is why this resource, *The*

Passion of the Christ: a Biblical Guide, is in your hands. We at Harvest Ministries developed this special biblical guide so believers in Christ will learn how to use this film to share their faith, or so you, as a reader, may come to know Jesus as your Lord and Savior.

So here's the plan for sharing the gospel of the Passion:

1. Use this resource to understand more about the people, the places, the politics, the prophecies, and most importantly, the gospel of the Passion.
2. Prepare to bring a nonbeliever by praying for the person you plan to invite.
3. Then, invite that unsaved friend or family member to the movie.
4. Give them a free copy of this biblical guide so they can use it as a "program" for the movie.
5. Take them to see the movie and offer to pay for their ticket.
6. Afterward, simply talk about the movie with them, praying and looking for opportunities to share about the life-changing message of Jesus Christ.

I am telling you, I believe people will come to Christ through this movie, because it is the perfect springboard for you to share the gospel. It is our prayer at Harvest Ministries that you will take advantage of *The Passion of The Christ,* along with this guide, to share His love with others.

HOW TO HAVE A RELATIONSHIP WITH JESUS CHRIST

Finally, if you desire to have a relationship with Christ or if you want to lead a friend or a family member to Christ, I want to share with you a few simple things you need to know:

First, realize that you are a sinner.

No matter how good a life we try to live, we still will fall miserably short of God's standards.

The Bible says, "No one is good—not even one" (Romans 3:10). Another word for *good* is *righteous*. The word *righteous* means "one who is as he or she ought to be." Apart from Jesus Christ, we cannot become the people we "ought to be."

Second, recognize that Jesus Christ died on the cross for you.

Scripture says, "But God showed His great love for us by sending Christ to die for us while we were still sinners" (Romans 5:8). God gave His very Son to die in our place when we least deserved it. As the Apostle Paul said, "[Christ] loved me and gave Himself for me . . ." (Galatians 2:20).

Third, repent of your sin.

The Bible tells us to "repent therefore and be converted" (Acts 3:19 NKJV). The word *repent* means to change our direction in life. Instead of running from God, we can run toward Him.

Fourth, receive Jesus Christ into your life.

Becoming a Christian is not merely believing some creed or going to church on Sunday. It is having Christ Himself take residence in your life and heart. Jesus said, " 'Behold, I stand at the door [of your life] and knock. If anyone hears My voice and opens the door, I will come in . . .' " (Revelation 3:20 NKJV).

Jesus stands at the door of your life right now and is knocking. He says that if you will hear His voice and open the door, He will come in. If you would like to know that when you die, you will go to heaven, and if you want to have a life that is full of purpose and meaning, then pray this suggested prayer and mean it with your heart:

∽∾

Dear Lord Jesus, I know I am a sinner. I believe You died for my sins and rose again from the dead. Right now, I turn from my sins and open the door of my heart and life. I confess You as my personal Lord and Savior. Thank you for saving me. Amen.